THEN & NOW

LABETTE COUNTY

OPPOSITE: Adam's Bluff is located southeast of Parsons on Labette Creek. For more than half a century, the bluff, which was named for landowner Ira F. Adams, was a popular picnic site. This group photograph was taken around 1905. (Historic image courtesy Parsons Historical Society Museum.)

THEN & NOW

LABETTE COUNTY

Mike Brotherton and David Mattox

This book is dedicated to the early photographers of Labette County.
Many of their names have faded from memory,
but the images they created are reminders of our past.

ISBN 978-0-7385-8292-4

Library of Congress Control Number: 2011927451

Published by Arcadia Publishing
Charleston, South Carolina

Printed in the United States of America

For all general information, please contact Arcadia Publishing:
Telephone 843-853-2070
Fax 843-853-0044
E-mail sales@arcadiapublishing.com
For customer service and orders:
Toll-Free 1-888-313-2665

Visit us on the Internet at www.arcadiapublishing.com

On the Front Cover: The first Armistice Day celebration held in Parsons was on November 11, 1930. On that day, two dedications took place. The first was the dedication of the Doughboy Statue on the northwest corner of the Parsons Municipal Building lawn. The second is pictured here. It was the dedication of a flagpole near Saint Patrick's Catholic Church. The construction of Saint Patrick's School in 1951 has slightly altered the view, but the original flagpole remains. (All cover images courtesy Parsons Historical Society Museum.)

On the Back Cover: Amateur Parsons photographer Charles Cadmus took this picture of young men enjoying a ride on the latest model of a horseless carriage around 1908. The west side of the second Missouri-Kansas-Texas (Katy) Railroad depot, the Victorian Depot, is in the background. A nearby spur of the railroad led to the International Harvester Building, where farm machinery and automobiles were unloaded.

Contents

Acknowledgments

This book would not have been possible without the generous support of several people and organizations. Roberta Grommet, Bill Wyckoff, and Elizabeth Turner were quick to loan us photographs, and Marla Yarbrough, Skip Smith, Don Alexander, and Bob Bartelli provided valuable material for some of the captions. Special thanks go to Bill Gorman and Don Dailey who provided access to photographs and information about the Kansas Army Ammunition Plant.

Many of the photographs in this book are from local museums in Chetopa, Oswego, and Mound Valley. All photographs not otherwise noted are from the Parsons Historical Society Museum. The authors received special assistance from the City of Altamont; the City of Parsons, especially, the Parsons Fire Department; the Oswego Public Library; Olson's Ace Hardware; the Labette County Road and Bridge Department; and Kanza Services.

We also gratefully acknowledge several previously published works. Maynard Harding's *The Katy Railroad & Parsons, Kansas: A Chronology*; Nelson Case's *History of Labette County and its Representative Citizens*; and William G. Cutler's *History of the State of Kansas* were indispensable resources that helped make this volume a reality. Centennial books about Altamont, Chetopa, Mound Valley, and Parsons also provided material, as did the unpublished manuscript of Sally Shaffer's study of life in early Labette County.

Finally, we thank family and friends who have, once again, given of their time and provided steady support for this project.

Introduction

Labette County covers 653.3 square miles in southeastern Kansas. That area is divided into 16 townships containing eight incorporated cities and five unincorporated places. Excluding state and federal highways, the county maintains 163 miles of asphalt, 971 miles of gravel, and 22 miles of dirt roads. It is also home to 65 cemeteries. Some, like Oakwood in Parsons, contain elaborate monuments to well-known pioneer families; other cemeteries are dotted with the distinctive white marble headstones once produced by the Oswego Marble Works.

The eastern half of the county is gently sloping countryside; the western half is made up of rolling hills punctuated with low mounds. The entire county is part of the Neosho River Valley, and two communities, Oswego and Chetopa, are built along the Neosho River, which begins near White City, Kansas, and runs for 460 miles before it empties into the Arkansas River in east-central Oklahoma. A number of creeks with colorful names—like Hackberry, Snow, Bachelor, and Pumpkin—as well as the better known Big Hill, Big and Little Labette, and Tolen complete the county's natural watershed system.

Although Labette County is known for its hunting, fishing, and recreational facilities, such as Pearson–Skubitz Big Hill Lake, it does not have the dramatic vistas common in the Flint Hills, 100 miles to the west, nor does it afford travelers the stark beauties of western Kansas. The county's charms are more subtle, its treasures revealed more slowly and, even then, most often to those with a keen eye and a willingness to explore its towns and county lanes. What most people find is a county comprised of productive farm and ranch land, a county with small towns that take pride in their pasts and work hard to guarantee their futures, and a county rich in history.

Labette County is the only county in Kansas bearing a name of French origin. On maps of the Southwest before 1830, Labette Creek was labeled *Riviere La Bete*. In fact, the first records of the area, dating from 1819, were kept in French. When the Osage Indians moved from Missouri and Arkansas to their new reservation in Kansas, many French families moved with them, intent on continuing their Indian trade.

Historical accounts agree that the county was named for the creek, but there are three hypotheses about the creek's name. Some site the name of French trapper Pierre La Baette who once lived near Chetopa. A more colorful theory involves the escapades of a group of French trappers who spotted a deer near their camp. The men chased and killed the deer and returned to camp to find that a skunk had visited, eaten their food, and left its unmistakable scent. The trappers shouted, "Oh, *la bete*! *La bete*!" or "Oh, the beast! The beast!" Another version of the same tale names an alligator as the transgressor. Others speculate that the Osage, who called the creek *En-gru-scah-op-pa*, are responsible for its name. That name translates to "the Beast" or "River of Reptiles."

When Kansas became a territory in 1854, the county boundaries on the state's eastern side had been established, including Dorn, present-day Neosho, and Labette Counties. Statehood in 1861 signaled a name change for the county to Neosho, and in 1867, the county was divided, becoming Neosho and Labette Counties. The selection of a Labette county seat was a hotly contested, politically charged decision, requiring multiple elections. Eventually, Oswego claimed the prize, beating out Montana in a close vote: 156 to 145.

As early as the 1870s, forward-thinking citizens were intent on capturing the county's past at a time when most devoted themselves to building its future. Nelson Case, W.A. Starr, and R.M. Donley founded the Labette County Historical Society in 1878, and Case published his *History of Labette County* in 1883.

Today, reminders of the county's colorful past are easy to find. Some are well known, others less obvious, but each offers its own rewards. Riverside Park, an 80-acre facility in Oswego, is perched on a bluff over 100 feet above the Neosho River. It offers the best views in Labette County. Thanks to the city's work and the help of the Oswego Parks and Community Foundation, Riverside is the epitome of a small town recreation area.

Mills Cemetery, a few hundred yards south of the junction of Rooks Road and US Highway 160, is perhaps the county's smallest cemetery, only 12 by 20 feet. Although it contains a single headstone, the well-cared-for site houses the graves of four early Labette County residents, the first buried in 1884. An elaborate wire fence encloses the space, which contains a single, ancient cedar.

Another gem is the long sidewalk that connects Edna with the Elm Grove Township and Edna Cemetery. The concrete walkway parallels State Highway 101 and features a small, ornate pedestrian bridge. It is easy to dismiss the traffic noises along the sidewalk and to remember a time when such a path was deemed a necessity. Its survival is testimony to the city's commitment to its citizens, both present and past.

Chetopa is famous for the great fishing that takes place near the low-water dam on the Neosho River. Although the sport is popular year-round, in early spring, anglers flock there to catch paddlefish, known locally as spoonbill. The nearby lowlands are home to the area's pecan groves that have earned Chetopa the title of "Pecan Capital of Kansas." Downtown, too, has its share of historic locations. The old mill near the Neosho River Bridge still commands respect, and the cottage-style, brick gas station complex on Maple Street is a rare example of roadside architecture.

No place in Labette County does a better job of evoking its past than the Southeast Kansas Farm History Center, located near the junction of US Highway 59 and US Highway 400 in Tolen Creek Park. The center's mission is to document, preserve, and demonstrate rural farm heritage and practices. The 1890s Stone House is the centerpiece of the complex, which offers excellent hiking trails that crisscross the creek. Special events bring out the crowds, but the real attraction is the opportunity to ponder the natural wonders of the area.

The 1884 edition of the Parsons City Directory describes Labette County as rich farming country and notes that "no part of Kansas has a more fertile soil, and a general failure of crops is unknown. It is well watered, and its railroad facilities are probably equal to those of any county in the State." The same volume describes its town and villages as lively places that keep pace with those of the other parts of the state and that are full of energetic citizens. Special praise went to Oswego: "It is well supplied with business blocks and some handsome residences. It has a thriving business trade and taken altogether may be considered as good a specimen of western towns as can be found."

Today, Labette County, Kansas, is a unique mix of people and places united by a common history. It is a place where people find beauty in everyday things, a place worth remembering, with a past worth revisiting. Its treasures are waiting to be rediscovered.

CHAPTER 1

OSWEGO

LITTLE TOWN

Oswego has been home to four mills, two of which were constructed in 1870. The first was steam powered; the second, on the Neosho River, was water driven. The Pearl Roller Mills was built in 1881 on the west edge of Oswego and soon gained a reputation for being one of the largest and best-equipped mills in the state.

Although the Oswego Opera House was dedicated in June 1879, it hosted its first major performance three months later: Gilbert and Sullivan's comic opera *H.M.S. Pinafore.* Originally designed to seat 450 people in the second-floor performance space, the opera house was later expanded to accommodate 1,000. By 1915, it was showing motion pictures, and its name had been changed to the Grand Theater. In its long service to the community, the opera house has been home to VFW dances and many commercial businesses. A recent renovation showcases the building's detailed facade and exemplifies the creative use of space for a new purpose. (Historic image courtesy Labette Bank.)

The most reprinted photograph of Robert O. Deming Sr. shows a confident man with a large mustache and a carnation pinned to the lapel of his well-tailored jacket. That image certainly suits Deming, perhaps the most successful of Oswego's early businessmen. Deming's home was constructed in the first years of the 20th century, and its stateliness is still very much in evidence. *A Standard History of Kansas and Kansans* calls the Deming Mansion "one of the finest homes in the state." The mansion, which began life at the 1904 Saint Louis World's Fair, was brought in boxcars to Oswego and reconstructed on its present site. (Historic image courtesy Roberta Grommet.)

What was once known as the "Brick Block" consists of 13 buildings on the west side of Commercial Street between Fourth and Fifth Streets. Constructed at a total cost of $60,000 in 1880 and 1881, all the second-story facilities were originally connected, a unique feature that created indoor traffic from one end of the block to the other. In the 1920s, Kingsbury and Frick's Drugstore occupied the north end of the block; however, the business was diversified, as illustrated by the banner over the pharmacy's entrance and the building's graphics. (Historic image courtesy Oswego Public Library.)

This turn-of-the-century harvest scene was taken at Fourth and Commercial Streets. Today, many of the city's original structures are still visible; most noticeable is the O. Gossard–Denton Hardware Building. Constructed in 1875, the building housed a variety of businesses until 1901, when Orcemus "Sim" Gossard opened his hardware store. Gossard's creative business sense, offering machinery on the installment plan and providing education to farmers on modern farming methods, proved popular. A mid-20th-century newspaper advertisement for the store exclaimed, "It is impossible to go wrong trading at Gossard's." In 1962, the business became Denton Hardware. (Historic image courtesy Roberta Grommet.)

The King Iron Bridge Manufacturing Company of Cleveland, Ohio, built the first bridge across the Neosho River in Oswego two years after the city had entered into an agreement with the company to build two bridges, with one north and another southeast of the city. Legal issues complicated the construction, and only the north bridge was built at a cost of $19,650. The first teams of horses crossed the bridge on November 27, 1874. The city donated the bridge to Labette County in 1886.

The 1949 ice storm paralyzed much of Labette County, including the city of Oswego. This photograph of the Carnegie Library shows the storm's effect. The city's library, one of 59 Carnegie public libraries in Kansas, was built in 1912 with $5,000 donated by the noted philanthropist. It was remodeled in 1965 and an addition was built in 1995, both of which were accomplished without compromising the architectural integrity of the original building. The Oswego Public Library was placed in the National Register of Historic Places in 1987. (Historic image courtesy Oswego Public Library.)

The Deming Investment Company Building was one of the largest commercial complexes in Oswego when it was completed in 1884. R.O. Deming Sr. was born in New York but grew up in Arkansas City, Kansas. After the family moved to Oswego in 1882, Deming turned his interest from hotel management to banking and, finally, to investment. His company helped develop land in Oklahoma Indian Territory and, after 1907, in the state of Oklahoma. The Oswego town well was located near the tree in front of the building. Progress claimed the well in 1920 when downtown streets were paved.

Built in 1939, the Oswego Hospital Building, which now houses the Southeast Kansas Education Museum, is one of the most distinctive buildings in Labette County. More at home in the Miami Beach Art Deco district than near Kansas wheat fields, it is, nonetheless, one of the architectural jewels of Oswego. With the possible exception of the Labette County Courthouse, no building in the city has such panache.

The Condon Bank operated in Oswego for 40 years, from 1882 until 1922. Like several other early prominent businessmen in Labette County, Charles Condon was born in New York. In 1868, at the age of 26, he moved to Oswego. Before his death in 1915, he owned banks throughout southeast Kansas and was the third-largest landowner in Kansas. The early-20th-century photograph of Commercial Street features an elegantly clad woman driving an automobile.

The facade of the Oswego "Bath House" has changed little since it was constructed in 1935. Like many other Depression-era public buildings, it was built by the Works Progress Administration, part of Franklin Roosevelt's New Deal recovery plan. Although the rooftop sun deck is now closed, the building retains its original charm, which is derived chiefly from the juxtaposition of it rough-hewn stones and its Art Deco styling. (Historic image courtesy Roberta Grommet.)

The Oswego House Hotel began as a log cabin on the corner of Fourth and Merchant Streets. By 1870, a frame structure had replaced the cabin, and in 1880, a two-story brick hotel was constructed. Ten years later, in 1890, the final additions to the pressed-brick hotel were made at a cost of $30,000. Advertisements for the hotel mention that stabling was available with the house. For many years, the hotel dining room offered special dinners on Thanksgiving, Christmas, and New Year's. It closed in 1975.

The Oswego Post Office, which was placed in the National Register of Historic Places in 1989, was dedicated on July 4, 1939. Before that time, postal services were offered at various storefront locations. One year after the Classical Revival–style building was completed, Robert E. Larter, a Topeka artist who taught at Washburn University, created a mural for the west wall of the lobby. *Farm Life* was funded by the US Treasury Department's Section of Fine Arts. It is one of only 27 post office murals in Kansas.

Three separate structures have served as the Labette County Courthouse since 1868. The first, a simple, frame building, was originally constructed as a public school by the citizens of Oswego who later donated the facility to the county. The second, built in 1880, featured an ornate cupola. It, too, was a gift to the county from public-minded townspeople; today's courthouse was built at taxpayers' expense in 1948 in the Art Moderne style. Its sleek, streamlined design is uncommon in Kansas courthouses.

CHAPTER 2

Chetopa

Catfish and Pecans

The photographer who created this image and wrote its description must have had a sense of humor, for the scene he captured in 1919 is far from quiet. Of special interest is the Golden Rule Store, one of a chain of mercantile stores which began in Wyoming in 1902. By 1912, there were 34 Golden Rule Stores. In 1913, the owner changed the store's name to J.C. Penney Company.

Col. Jeremiah B. Cook's elaborate Italianate home was completed in 1875. Cook, who was born in Pennsylvania, was one of the best-known figures in Labette County at the time, a pioneer whose life story reads like an adventure novel. By the time he arrived in Chetopa at age 36, he had been a flatboat hand, a gold miner in California (he traveled to and from California via the Isthmus of Panama), a cotton plantation manager, and the commander of the 3rd United States African American Cavalry Regiment during the Civil War. (Historic image courtesy Chetopa Historical Society Museum.)

The Neosho Valley Investment Company was established in March 1885. One of its founders, John W. Breidenthal, was later appointed bank commissioner of Kansas. In 1900, he ran for governor of Kansas as both the Democratic and Populist parties' candidate. By 1905, the impressive investment company building at the corner of Fourth and Maple Streets housed the city's post office. Then, as well as now, the elaborate stained glass, arched windows are the building's crown jewels.

The Chetopa Baptist Church was established on May 1, 1869. Under the leadership of Rev. A.C. Bateman, the eight-member congregation made plans in 1870 to erect a church at a cost of $3,300. Construction took place in the spring and summer of that year, and the building was dedicated on August 14. The present facility is much expanded, but the arched, engraved stone above the entrance to the old church remains visible in the remodeled building. It reads, "First Baptist Church 1869–1947."

The City Electric Light Company originally burned coal to create the steam that generated the plant's power. Water for the process and to supply the city's general needs came from the nearby Neosho River. In 1899, publicity for the facility noted that the plant produced enough electricity to light 900 incandescent bulbs. Today, the city's power comes from the Empire District Electric Plant in Riverton, Kansas.

Riggs Drugstore has been a fixture of downtown since 1923, but the building itself has housed a pharmacy for more than 100 years. In April 2010, Riggs opened its new facility two blocks east of the old building on the corner lot once home to the Chetopa Opera House. The move marked the end of an era for the old building, but the pharmacy's new facility features a soda fountain in homage to its previous location.

This recently constructed memorial at Ninth and Maple Streets contains the original cornerstone of the Sacred Heart Catholic Church, which once stood at this location. A brick church replaced the first church, a wooden-frame structure, in 1900, and stained glass windows were added to the building in 1930. In May 2008, the church was declared unsafe, and the Diocese of Wichita closed it shortly thereafter. Bricks from the church were used to create the memorial, and the stained glass windows were installed in the Mother of God Church in Oswego.

Sig Lehman was one of Chetopa's most well-known business and civic leaders. He served as mayor for almost a quarter of a century, from 1907 until 1916 and then again from 1919 until 1932. Lehman's Star Store carried a wide range of merchandise, some of which can be seen hanging in front of the store above the two hitch racks. The east half of the block was destroyed by fire, and the Chetopa State Bank and Trust Building now occupies the site.

The west side of Chetopa's main street was home to three service stations when this Rexall drugstore postcard image was produced in the late 1950s. All three were still in business in 1976, but only two of the structures remain today, each housing another type of business; a modern convenience store–gasoline station occupies the third site. A sign in front of the old Phillips 66 Service Station advertises gas for 24¢ per gallon.

Four bridges have spanned the Neosho River at Chetopa. The second and fourth bridges are pictured here. The first was constructed in 1875 at a cost of $10,000. The second bridge was completed in 1909 and the third in 1939. The current span, named Veteran's Memorial Bridge, was dedicated in 2009. Before the first bridge was built, ferries charged the following rates: 10¢ for one man on foot; 75¢ for one team of four horses, mules, or oxen; 10¢ each for cattle; 5¢ for hogs and sheep; and 50¢ for a two-horse buggy.

CHAPTER 3

PARSONS

QUEEN CITY OF THE SOUTHWEST

The Parsons Crystal Ice Company was one of at least four ice companies that operated in Parsons. Before scientists produced synthetic refrigerants in the 1920s, ice wagons were a common sight on city streets. However, by the late 1940s, most homes had electric refrigerators and old-fashioned "iceboxes" were a thing of the past. Early advertisements for the company claim the following: "There is no substitute for ice; it saves food and insures health."

On June 15, 1905, the Missouri-Kansas-Texas Railroad announced that a new railroad shop, the largest west of the Mississippi River, would be built in Parsons. Two years later, on July 25, 1907, the project was completed. "The shops" were 150 feet wide and 860 feet long . They contained 129,000 square feet and were constructed at a cost of $290,000. Today, the structure is as impressive as it was more than 100 years ago. Kanza Services, a private company, now operates a railcar repair shop in the facility.

The doughboy statue on the Municipal Building lawn, officially titled *The Spirit of the America Doughboy*, has been a fixture in Parsons since its dedication on November 11, 1930. The statue was designed by E.M. Viquesney of Spencer, Indiana, in 1921. Although most of Viquesney's statues are bronze, Parsons's doughboy is made of Italian marble and is considered rare. At least 136 identical doughboys exist, scattered over 35 states. Only three, however, reside in Kansas.

The gates to Oakwood Cemetery, the city's oldest cemetery, have changed little since they were completed in November 1911. A gift from the Daughters of the American Revolution, the imposing stone-and-iron structure was dedicated "In memory of the revolutionary ancestors of Hannah Jameson." That dedication explains the date of 1776 in the older photograph. A contemporary account of the dedication ceremony notes that the gateway cost $640 and was "a magnificent and fitting entrance to Parsons's city of the dead."

Floral tributes mark a family grave in Oakwood Cemetery. The photograph, taken in the 1920s, captures a small section of the historic cemetery where many of Parsons's pioneer families are buried. Robert S. Stevens, often cited as the man who guided much of the early growth of Parsons, presented 20 acres to the city to be used as a cemetery soon after the Parsons Town Company was formed on October 17, 1870.

The Grand Army of the Republic, a national organization designed to help Civil War veterans and their families, organized a chapter in Parsons on June 2, 1882, Antietam Post No. 64. In 1886, the group purchased land in Oakwood Cemetery, and by 1895, eighty-four soldiers had been buried there. Improvements—including the addition of two eight-inch Columbiad cannons, concrete abutments, bronze statues, and a gazebo—were eventually added. A total of 375 headstones now mark the graves of Civil War veterans.

Parsons has seen its share of celebrity visits, including Rutherford B. Hayes, Ulysses S. Grant, and W.T. Sherman, but few notables have come to town with more commercial fanfare than did Buffalo Bill Cody and Pawnee Bill. Like his more famous partner, Pawnee Bill was a Wild West showman, who, in 1907, created a "Far East" show that featured Japanese performers, Pawnee Indians, Mexican cowboys, and Arab jugglers. Cody and Bill joined forces in 1908. They were in Parsons for one performance, on Thursday, October 7, 1909. (Historic image courtesy Roberta Grommet.)

Studio Grand took several photographs of downtown Parsons in October 1909. This one, which shows the 1700 block of Main Street, captures the elaborate decorations on display at the Kress Store. The original Kress Building was destroyed in the 1907 fire, which consumed the Baptist church and most of a two-block area on Main Street and Washington Avenue. The four-story building at the end of the block is the Strasburger Building, itself a victim of fire in 1918. (Historic image courtesy Roberta Grommet.)

Although only a few remain in use as private residences, for many years, apartment houses lined a section of Sixteenth Street in Parsons, especially between Washington and Belmont Avenues. Family members pose on their second-story balcony for this photograph, probably taken in the early 1920s. The structure has been modernized, but it is easy to see that the two structures are the same.

Dr. A.F. Neeley, who served as mayor of Parsons from 1889 until 1891, built the house on the southeast corner of Seventeenth Street and Broadway Avenue. However, it was greatly expanded and remodeled by Lewis and Charlette Graves in 1900. Graves, a successful businessman and contractor, died that same year of self-inflicted knife wounds. The structure later belonged to J.M. Gregory, who, for many years, operated a funeral and furniture business at 1806 Main Street, the Gregory Building. Later, Joseph and Anna Carson operated Carsons Funeral Home at this site.

The first interurban car, a part of the Union Traction–Electric Railway Line, arrived in Parsons on Saturday, December 21, 1912. This photograph, which looks northwest, shows one of the cars on Main Street. It was taken from the roof of Parsons High School, which was then located at the corner of Twenty-sixth and Main Streets, an area considered the western edge of the city at that time. Before settlers planted trees on the surrounding prairie, it was possible to see for miles from such a vantage point.

McKinley Grade School was built in 1935 as part of the Federal Works Agency. An all-school project documented its construction; students wrote daily progress reports and took weekly photographs. Then, they created two scrapbooks, putting together what is probably the most detailed construction report of any public building in Parsons. Among a host of congratulatory greetings is one from Marguerite LeHand, Pres. Franklin Roosevelt's private secretary for 21 years. McKinley School closed in the 1980s, survived the 2000 tornado, and now serves as a place of worship.

Texas-bound train No. 5 passes under the manual interlocking signal bridge that was located just north of Appleton Avenue. The Missouri-Kansas-Texas Railroad installed the bridge in the 1920s to control train movements out of Parsons to the west and south. Freight trains received their orders here, while passenger trains received orders at the depot. The signal bridge, which was rare and represented a large investment of money and maintenance, was removed shortly after passenger service was discontinued in 1965.

Parsons's first water tower, originally called a standpipe, was one of the largest in Kansas when it was constructed in 1892, north of Saint Patrick's Catholic Church. The tower pictured here was built in 1963. Advertisements produced at the time touted the 500,000-gallon "Waterspheriod" located near Appleton Avenue and the Missouri-Kansas-Texas Railroad tracks. The old tower now carries the city's name; the two newer ones publicize the Labette Community College Cardinals and the Parsons High School Vikings.

A total of 139 years separates these two photographs, both of which capture Main Street looking east from the corner of Main Street and Central Avenue. The 1872 photograph is one in a series of photographs taken of "the Infant Wonder of the West" only a year after the city was incorporated. The Knights of Columbus Building once housed the Kansan Theater, a 1920s movie house with an impressive, Spanish-styled facade.

The Urban Renewal Project of the late 1960s drastically changed the look of many city blocks in downtown Parsons. This photograph shows the block west of the underpass on Main Street as demolition was underway. It offers one of the last views of the Interurban Building and the West Theater. Labette Bank modeled its new headquarters on the Victorian Katy Station. Its interpretation of the original building was so successful that many first-time visitors to Parsons think the bank occupies the actual depot. (Historic image courtesy Ken Ervin.)

As a conduit to the Katy Station, Broadway Avenue was once Parsons's main business thoroughfare, more so than Main Street. This photograph, taken shortly before urban renewal began, captures several businesses that are fondly remembered: the Broadway Café, the Arcade, and, especially, Newkirk's Music Store. One Parsons baby boomer, Jayna Henderson, remembers spending Saturday afternoons browsing 45-rpm records. New releases were 99¢ and records that had been recently removed from jukeboxes around town were sale priced at 49¢.

The Parsons Motor Car Co. was located at Central and Washington Avenues. Besides offering garage services and a curbside air pump, the company sold Goodrich tires and Dodge Brothers cars. The small sign located in the intersection reminded motorists to keep to the right. In a new building, Alloway's Cobblestone Restaurant drew customers to the location until the late 1980s. Later, Ernesto's moved to the building. When the structure was destroyed in the 2000 tornado, the owners expanded and rebuilt the restaurant.

Elam Cleaners operated at 1816 Broadway for nearly two decades, during the 1940s and 1950s. Its Art Deco–inspired signage, complete with neon lighting, was cutting-edge at the time. The interior of the building was just as modern. Curved walls and recessed, indirect lighting added glamour to the customer service area. Today, the building retains a more classic look, but the business it houses is state of the art.

Seventeenth Street, looking south from Main Street, was one of the most popular scenes in Parsons for early-day photographers. It is no wonder, for few Southeast Kansas cities possessed a more striking town center. An addition on the south side of the post office has changed the view somewhat, and the lawn of the Municipal Building has fewer trees. However, the vista continues to impress.

Two of the most distinctive buildings in downtown Parsons look much the same as they did 100 years ago. Both were constructed by Charles H. Kimball, a two-term state senator who fought to bring the State Hospital to Parsons. The Edwards-Kimball Building, 1801–1803 Main Street, originally housed White's Furniture. Now, it is leased by SKIL, an independent living resource center. Across the street, the Kimball Building currently houses a variety of businesses at street level and apartments above.

The Parsons Water Company, a private company, completed the city's first water system in July 1884. Labette Creek Dam was central to the enterprise. Located on Big Labette Creek north of town, the dam created the reservoir where steam-powered pumps were used to bring water to Parsons. Initially, the city paid $3,000 a year to the company for 50 hydrants. Unfortunately, the system was soon deemed unsatisfactory, and water came to Parsons from the Neosho River. When Lake Parsons was created in the 1950s, Labette Creek once again became the primary water source for Parsons.

Members of the Parsons Gold Star Mothers Organization were honored guests at the dedication of the World War II memorial on the southwest corner of the Parsons Municipal Building lawn in 1950. The Gold Star Mothers Organization began in 1918 and became a national organization in 1928. The local Parsons chapter was responsible for the construction of the memorial, which features panels dedicated to each branch of the armed forces. Each Veterans Day, a floral gold star graces the monument.

The exterior of the Parsons Municipal Building has changed little in the last 88 years, although angle parking has replaced parallel parking on Seventeenth Street. However, the interior of the building has received periodic face-lifts, the most extensive of which was the auditorium renovation. In 1974, the city closed the auditorium, citing safety issues. A grassroots movement in the 1980s led to its renovation, and the auditorium reopened in March 1989. Since that time, almost half a million people have attended events there.

Douglass School, Parsons's only African American elementary school, was constructed in 1908 at 822 South Central Avenue. An addition, which included a gymnasium and an auditorium, was completed in 1925. Douglass housed first through eighth grades; later, junior high classes were added to the curriculum. In 1938, the Douglass Panthers earned statewide recognition when the basketball team captured the Kansas Negro League Championship. Between 1955 and 1958, classes were phased out, and the school closed in 1958.

The State Bank of Parsons Building, constructed in 1904, was only a few years old when this photograph was taken. The buildings north of the State Bank were replaced by the "new" First National Bank Building in 1923. Years later, the bank's impressive Classical styling was hidden by a 1960s reflective, glass facade. The 2000 tornado swept away the glass panels, and citizens rediscovered its original beauty.

The Kress Store in Parsons was one of hundreds of five-and-dime stores opened by Samuel H. Kress, beginning in 1896. Kress thought of his stores as public art that would contribute to the overall landscape of the community. Although the architecture of the Parsons store was less elaborate than many of his buildings, it did contain the characteristic curved-glass display windows and the Kress insert in front of both entrances.

The Elks Theater, later renamed the Orpheum, cost $65,000 when it was built in 1904. It served as a movie theater until 1939, when it was destroyed by fire. Plans for a hotel on the "Orpheum Corner" were in the making as early as 1942. That fall, the *Parsons Sun* announced that a seven-story hotel, designed in the new International style, was slated for the site. However, funding for the project was not secured, and the lot remained vacant until 1954, when the Parsonian Hotel opened.

Bob Bartelli was seven years old in 1948 when he posed for this photograph standing in front of a fleet of delivery trucks at his father's bakery. Two years earlier, his father, Joe Bartelli, had opened the Sally Ann Bread Company. Over the years, there has been much speculation about the ornate terra-cotta emblem on the front of the building. When he posed for the recent photograph, 63 years later, Bartelli solved the mystery: its only purpose is decorative. (Historic image courtesy Bob Bartelli.)

Employees of the J.B. McElhaney Crystal Ice Company pose for a photograph at Marvel Park Stadium. The current stadium and sports complex are relatively new additions to the park, which was created on land donated to the city by local businessmen in the 1880s. Long before this 1940s photograph was taken, horse-drawn ice wagons had disappeared from Parsons's streets. Today, the same setting serves as a backdrop for another group: members of the city's public works–utilities crew.

Today, Marvel Park is known for its sports facilities, but for many years, its chief attraction was its large oval track, which was often used for racing. Horses, motorcycles, and automobiles once competed for honors at the park, also home to the Tri-State Fair during the 1920s and 1930s. The present park stadium dates from the late 1930s. The flagstone fence that borders the park's north and east sides was constructed by the Works Progress Administration.

The Forest Park Gazebo was built in El Dorado Springs, Missouri, but it was moved to Parsons in 1904, where it quickly became one of the most popular gathering spots in the park. The two-tiered, all-wooden structure was the site for city celebrations, family gatherings, and dances. It burned in the 1940s; in 2008, the Seaton Family Pavilion was dedicated in honor of longtime Parsons music teacher Norma Jean Seaton. The pavilion is the site of the popular summer concert series and other special events, such as this Fourth of July program. (Now image courtesy David Beach.)

Ervin's Garage opened in Parsons in 1911. Although it was once located on Washington Avenue and, later, on Broadway Avenue, when this photograph was taken, it had moved to the heart of downtown Parsons at 1720–1722 Main Street. A three-generation family business, Ervin's operated for 94 years, a distinction that few commercial enterprises can match. Some photographs of this building show a miniature automobile mounted on the top ledge of the building's brick facade.

By all accounts, the Angell Matthewson house was the finest residence in Parsons. It was located on the south side of the 1500 block of Morgan Avenue. Matthewson, an early businessman and investor, built the largest hotel in town in 1886. Originally from New York, Matthewson served for three years in the Civil War before he moved to Kansas at the urging of his friend Judge Levi Parsons. After Matthewson's death, the home was dismantled and divided into three separate residences, only one of which survives and is located on North Sixteenth Street.

The Parsons Post Office Building will celebrate its 100th anniversary in 2012. Before the current facility was constructed, the post office had storefront locations, first, in the Edwards Opera House Building at 1828 Broadway Avenue and, later, at 1812 Main Street. Two years before the city was incorporated, in 1869, a postal station, known by the town's first name, Mendota, was located in a store near the local mill. (Historic image courtesy Roberta Grommet.)

In the 1920s, members of the Parsons Fire Department posed for a series of photographs on Washington Avenue. In 1936, with help from the Public Works Administration, a New Deal recovery plan, the city built a new fire station on the same site. It features a marble-clad entryway, terrazzo floors, an interior skylight, and a three-story tower where fire hoses are hung to dry. Early 1900s photographs hang in the building, including one of Louie the dog, the department's mascot in 1911.

The Parsons Foundry and Machine Works was located at 2031 Grand Avenue. In the 1901 Parsons City Directory, E.M. Haubold is listed as proprietor. An advertisement for the company boasted that the foundry produced "all kinds of casting and machine works done in first-class style." It also noted that mail orders were welcome and promised that they would receive prompt attention. Alexander's was established by Melvin Alexander in 1927. The company moved to the location pictured in 1930 and to its industrial park location in 2003.

The Carnegie Library, which celebrated its centennial in 2009, has served as a backdrop for many special events. During World War II, patriotic Parsonians turned out to see the two-man Japanese submarine that toured the United States as a promotion for war bond sales. The vest-pocket submarine, officially the HA-19, was captured on December 8, 1941, on the island of Oahu, Hawaii. It was 81 feet long and weighed 40 tons. Citizens who purchased war bonds or stamps were allowed an interior view, where they saw two mannequins dressed as Japanese crew.

The Mathis Hatchery and Feed Store, located in the 1800 block of Washington Street, was a thriving business from the mid-1930s until the mid-1950s. After the business closed, Ace Hardware opened at the location, and the brick building east of the hatchery became the Eagles Lodge. According to first-hand reports, the hatchery building retained "the smell of chickens" for several years, especially during damp weather. Both buildings were destroyed in the April 2000 tornado. Ace Hardware now occupies the area east of the Parsons Fire Department Building.

The Missouri-Kansas-Texas Railroad celebrated its 75th anniversary in 1945. The weeklong diamond jubilee celebration was the biggest event in Parsons's history; a crowd estimated at 10,000 greeted the old-fashioned train that carried Katy railroad officials to town. One of the week's highlights was the hour-long parade, which boasted over 3,000 parade participants and stretched for two miles along Main Street. More than 25,000 people crowded downtown to view the event.

Don and Doris Brenner opened their pharmacy in downtown Parsons, on the southwest corner of Eighteenth and Main Streets, in 1950. By 1961, they had remodeled the front porch of a home in the 1500 block of Main Street and created a modern, drive-through facility. It remained until 2007 when the structure was demolished to make way for the new Bowen Pharmacy. In the rare nighttime photograph taken shortly after Brenners had completed the remodeling, Friskie, the chihuahua, guards the store after hours.

The Seventh Day Adventist Church Building, which was located at 401 North Sixteenth Street, is a fine example of a repurposed building. Instead of demolishing an existing structure, its current owner chose the "three Rs:" redesign, refurbish, and remodel. The building also serves as a reminder of how quickly elements of a cityscape can change. Only two years separate these photographs.

CHAPTER 4

ALTAMONT
SMALL TOWN PRIDE

Altamont celebrated its centennial in 1984, more than 60 years after this photograph of the Rust Lumber Company was taken. Fast-growing catalpa trees were prized for their large, heart-shaped leaves that provided deep shade at a time when mature trees were rare and timbered lands were confined to areas near the Neosho River and the creeks of Labette County.

Although the city's bandstand and the well beneath it have disappeared from the north end of Main Street, several historic structures remain along the thoroughfare. The Baker garage, owned by brothers Charlie, Cyrus, and Jim, looks much the same as it did when the building was the Ford service center. The decorative brickwork along the top facade and above the windows and doors illustrates the attention to detail that builders once gave to structures intended for utilitarian use. (Historic image courtesy City of Altamont.)

The Farmer's Cooperative Elevator Company was established in 1918; the company held its first annual meeting to elect a board of directors on May 8, 1919. At the time, the board determined the manager's salary, $100 a month. In the decades that followed, the cooperative added the following to its holdings: a hammermill in 1930, a lumberyard in 1931, and a service station in 1959. Even though the facade of the original structure has changed, the cooperative is easy to recognize, chiefly by the placement of its windows and doors. (Historic image courtesy City of Altamont.)

The United Methodist Church was first housed in a frame structure, which was completed in 1883. The congregation had outgrown its first facility 25 years later. Published records indicated that the present church was constructed at a cost of $8,000 and dedicated in June 1909. However, the caption of the historic photograph indicates a projected price that is double that amount. In 1922, a parsonage was added to the property. Until 1953, the church used on-site wells for its water supply. (Historic image courtesy Bill Wyckoff.)

In 1893, a special act of the Kansas legislature established the Labette County High School to be located in Altamont. Despite local opposition to the accompanying tax levy, the state supreme court upheld the legislative action, and the school was constructed at a cost of $23,805. When it was dedicated on May 4, 1895, it was one of the most impressive buildings in the county. The two-story Romanesque-styled structure dominated the cityscape and towered over the surrounding treeless plains. (Historic image courtesy Bill Wyckoff.)

Labette County High School has appeared on postcards since the school was built. This view, which looks east, was taken approximately 20 years after it was constructed on the "hill" that early settlers thought was the highest point in the area. In its long history, the school system has often been in the limelight. In 1964, it was named one of the three outstanding high schools in the United States. In 1968, *Look* magazine published a feature article on the school system, and a Labette County High School co-ed graced its cover. (Historic image courtesy Bill Wyckoff.)

CHAPTER 5

LABETTE COUNTY

TOWN AND COUNTRY VIEWS

Mound Valley's Bush Hotel, originally known as the Commercial Hotel, was constructed by Robert Campbell, who served as its first proprietor. It was located on Main Street, just one block north of the flagpole. Before it was torn down in 1940, the hotel had been owned and operated by five different families. (Historic image courtesy Roberta Grommett.)

Charles A. Bradbury opened a livery stable in Mound Valley in 1892, but in 1917, the stable was torn down to make way for a Ford service station, which eventually became a dealership. For many years, Bradbury's was known for its customer service. During its October 1957 new car promotion, the company presented prospective women buyers with orchids, which were flown from Hawaii for the event. When the business closed in 1959, it was one of the oldest Ford dealerships in the nation. The Mound Valley Maintenance Department now occupies the site. (Historic image courtesy Mound Valley Historical Society.)

The Mound Valley State Bank Building was constructed in 1906, the same year the city's telephone company began service. On January 10, 1912, the bank was destroyed by fire, which began in a second-story storage area utilized by another business. The blaze was one of three that struck downtown that week. When the bank's vice president announced plans for a new facility, he noted the following: "We will have no tenants and will construct a one-story building." Today, the structure is home to the Mound Valley Historical Museum. (Historic image courtesy Mound Valley Historical Society.)

The First National Bank and the Hulen's Opera House occupied the north side of the street where the old Township Community Center now stands in Mound Valley. Doctor Huff, a cancer specialist, maintained an office above the bank. The block burned in 1907 and was rebuilt in 1908. The community center opened in May 1941 with great fanfare, including a concert featuring the A.J. Cripe Cowboy Band. The local newspaper reported that the building's dedication "packed the town with a good-natured, happy, and well-behaved throng." (Historic image courtesy Mound Valley Historical Society.)

At 6:00 a.m. on January 28, 1924, the first power produced at the Kansas Gas and Electric Company Plant was released. The complex cost $8 million, and its 355-foot smokestack—said at the time to be the tallest in the United States—soon became a county landmark. Six hundred and sixty-four transmitter towers—each 84 feet tall—were built between the plant and Wichita, which received the bulk of the energy produced at the facility on the Neosho River.

Located in Hackberry Township and served by the Missouri Pacific Railroad, Bartlett was named for its founder and ardent promoter, Robert A. Bartlett. The plat of the town was filed with the county's register of deeds on June 5, 1886, although the township had been formed almost two decades before when its first county officers were elected in April 1867. Bartlett's first residence was built by B.F. Fox, who also ran the town's first blacksmith shop.

The facade of Bartlett's Farmers Store remains much the same as it was when it was constructed in 1920. While the structure's overall style is strictly utilitarian, its detailed signage is unusual. Both the date and letters are relief-carved stone and are as impressive today as they were when they were produced more than 90 years ago. When the store was built, Bartlett's population was near 250. (Historic image courtesy Bill Wyckoff.)

The first building on the site of what was to become Edna was an 11-by-14-foot general store owned by Jeptha Lackey. It opened in 1876, but the town was not platted until August 1886. One year later, C.T. Ewing, who was associated with banks in Thayer and Cherryvale, opened the International Bank of Edna. The stone structure survived the city's two most destructive fires, one in 1889 and the other in 1891, and today, it houses the Edna Historical Society Museum.

Pleasant Hill Cemetery, located six miles west of Parsons near Dennis, is one of dozens of rural cemeteries in Labette County. Many of the older tombstones, the earliest of which date from 1872, display elaborately carved Victorian symbols. Among those buried at Pleasant Hill are Civil War soldiers from Indiana, Illinois, and Pennsylvania. The photograph from the mid-1920s shows a groundskeeper with a cylinder reel mower and a larger cylinder model pulled by a horse.

Thanks to the efforts of Sen. Clyde Reed Sr. and the Parsons Chamber of Commerce, work began on building the Kansas Ordnance Plant in Parsons on August 1941. Despite heavy rains—amounting to over 23 inches in September and October 1941—that delayed construction, the plant was completed in 1942 at a cost of approximately $24 million, which was $4 million under the original estimate. Building No. 52 housed one of two fire stations that served the facility. (Historic image courtesy Kansas Army Ammunition Plant.)

The historic photograph of the "10 hundred line" was taken at 11:00 a.m. on April 21, 1942, looking east. The plant's original mission to provide munitions and materials for European and American forces during World War II was made possible by the thousands of workers who built the facility. Between 10,000 and 12,000 people worked an astounding 14 million hours to finish the construction in little over a year. (Historic image courtesy Kansas Army Ammunition Plant.)

The first plans for many of the plant's buildings—more than 700 spread over 13,700 acres—called for air-conditioned, brick structures with slate roofs. Citing economic factors, officials changed those plans, and many buildings, including the Administration Building and dormitories, were constructed of wood. Others, as this close-up of a loading dock on the nine hundred line shows, were built of structural clay tile. The plant also housed water, power, and sewage facilities, a hospital, a locomotive repair shop, and a cafeteria that seated 525. (Historic image courtesy Kansas Army Ammunition Plant.)

Minus the installment of the long evacuation slides, the Melt Load Building retains the same silhouette today as it did as workers finished the facility in 1942. During World War II production, the plant earned four "E" Awards, which were service awards given to outstanding government institutions. In 1963, the Kansas Ordnance Plant became the Kansas Army Ammunition Plant, and in March 2009, it ended its munitions production mission after 68 years. The Great Plains Industrial Park now occupies the site. (Historic image courtesy Kansas Army Ammunition Plant.)

MAP SEARCH